COACHING HABITS:

HOW TO TOTALLY CHANGE YOUR LIFE FOREVER AND ACHIEVE SUCCESS

Table of Contents

Introduction

You learn the essential elements of coaching to help you take your achievement, and, where you can apply, that of others around you or your team, to the next level. We will work on knowing what questions to ask, how to set accountability goals and how to ensure that the process is active. You will also learn not only how to ask the appropriate questions but also how to listen to the answers given.

Most importantly, a life coach cannot professionally guide you through a sticky situation or a rough time if they have never experienced struggles themselves. A life coach can be considered good, if he or she has a positive outlook on life, and practically applies it.

If you want to be a life coach, but you freak out when you think that someone has grabbed your parking spot, but advise her clients that divorce can be a helpful step to grow personally, you are not genuine. Faking positive outlook will not help your client.

Another essential factor that life coach should take care is how he is organizing his life. If you say to your client that you will call, but you fail to do so, then it is a red flag that he is not entirely in control of his life, and should probably not be entrusted with your life.

All life coaches should be appropriately licensed. Your advice to your client could make or break his life. Hence, it is crucial for a life coach to be knowledgeable and well-trained in this promising career.

Thank you for buying this book, I hope it will answer all your questions on coaching habits.

Chapter 1: What is coaching?

Supposing you heard this:

During that period, he made me recite the multiplication tables such that I could even say them in reverse order. He also helped me in other subjects.

During that period, he got me to learn the multiplication tables; do the rest of my homework in time; ensure my uniform is ready to wear come morning and go to bed no later than 10 pm every day.

Which of the above two would you call coaching, and which one would you call tutoring?

Wow! We usually do not give much thought to these things, do we? Let us say, when it comes to tutoring, it is more concentrated on teaching facts and the how-to stuff; sometimes getting to drilling. But when it comes to coaching, it is an all-around business. Your coach wants to help you set the right environment for working or for doing whatever else is in question, even as you get assistance in gaining knowledge and skills.

So clearly, number 1 above is about tutoring, while number 2 is geared towards coaching.

Is that why sports coaches sometimes come across as father figures – or big brothers?

The answer is yes – that is precisely the reason. Coaches will not just show you how to do things, but they will also push you to try your limit. They are still comfortable nosing around to understand your social life, and in that respect, it does not pass as being nosy, as it is their business to know the characters you are associating with and the impact they are having on your mindset.

Sports coaches are famous. What else is coachable?

Oh –virtually everything! We have just mentioned how a coach helps you set the right working environment. So, if you are learning music, for example, and you pay for tuition classes, what you should expect is to determine the notes; the extent to which you open your mouth to release certain A-s and O-s; and that kind of thing.

But when you go out for a music coach, the guy is going to teach you the foods and drinks that you should spare your gullet; the growling you should avoid no matter how upset someone makes you; how you should behave towards your colds; and such other things that are likely to have an impact on your voice box, your lungs, and all the other organs associated with release of sounds. Of course, this is not exclusive of the music skills. You will also be learning the necessary singing and instrumental skills.

Can you carry out coaching in the office?

In knowing those challenges, they then make suggestions on how those issues could be tackled. In the process, the individuals or groups come up with different scenarios and possible outcomes.

Ultimately, it is the employees themselves that make their pick. So, for a coach in the office, the responsibility is to help employees get into the mode of critical thinking – where they feel obliged to look for solutions; helping them take full charge of their role.

Chapter 2: Laying the Ground for Coaching

Do you want to be a great coach? One thing you need to appreciate is that the only way you are going to make headway in any field is if the environment is conducive. Otherwise, you will be running against a strong wind that counters most, if not all, of your efforts. That is not to undermine your competence and all, but really, whatever you have in your package will only benefit the person you are coaching if they are receptive.

Then again, you need to appreciate that for coaching to go well, both the coach and the person being coached need to be ready for it. And for sure, what strides can the coach make if the person being coached has no idea what coaching is all about?

Here is what everyone involved needs to know from the onset:

Be clear about what to expect from the coach
Coaching is not an ultimatum

Within the working environment, you need to make the employees understand that the coach is meant to help them deliver on their goals better and not to train them on how to do their job. If an employee is set to take on a new position, the understanding would be that the coach will prepare that employee to handle new responsibilities, which may be somewhat different from what they have always dealt with.

If the air is not cleared from the onset, the employees may have the perception that the coach has been sent to them to gather information and then provide feedback to management. And most likely, they will suspect that such information is to be used to assess those the organization needs to lay off.

Of course, with that mindset, the employees being coached are unlikely to be sincere and open. In fact, they may even hold back some information, including challenges that they face in performing their duties. So, bluntly speaking, the coach is neither an inspector nor a witch hunter, and you need to make that crystal clear from the beginning.

Coaching is provided as a continuing support service

It is vital that coaching is seen as a tool to help employees in their skill development and career in general. That means it is not helpful to have coaching being initiated just when everyone has condemned the section as failing. The minute management brings in a coach and the employees get the feeling the move is another way of saying shape up, or you are out of here, not much progress will be forthcoming.

Of course, what may have triggered the need for a coach could be poor performance, but the effort needs to be made to ensure the people being coached do not view the move as being either punitive or a threat.

Coaching is not meant to pre-empt legal action

If something needed to be done by management and was not done at the appropriate time, it is not reasonable that coaching should be used to camouflage the failure. If that is seen to be the case, or if the perception is that coaching is being provided to pre-empt legal action of sorts, the resources being used in this process will just be wasted; the coaching will not be helpful to either party.

Coaching needs to be supportive rather than remedial

Once you make coaching something that you do primarily to salvage a desperate situation, you will find yourself handling matters when essential relationships have already suffered. As such, the coaching may not be beneficial. As a matter of practice, it is best to carry out coaching at the earliest convenience.

Employ a coach from relevance

What is the coach's expertise?

Do you find a retired professional basketball player coaching athletics? Inevitably no – it would raise eyebrows, and justifiably so. In the same vein, it does not seem logical that you should hire a salesperson to coach an employee looking to take on a managerial position. You need a coach with the relevant expertise plus reasonable experience. And while trying to establish the coach's suitability, making a few calls to references is part of the bargain.

Is the coach's style suitable?

Please do not go looking for a suitable style because there cannot be a single one. It all depends on the person being coached. If, for instance, you are coaching people who have been delivering results by experience, having a young coach with big ideas on the science behind performance may not create a great relationship. On the contrary, you need a coach, young or old, who has the art of handling people in a fair manner.

In short, the coach needs to be flexible enough to be able to earn the trust of the people being coached. The coach's style should enable a relationship of mutual respect as well as confidence.

Be on the same page with the coach

Do not send a coach blindly – lay out the context

A coach will be helpful to the person being coached and to the organization as well if only full disclosure is made on the reason the coaching is necessary. For example, someone being coached in preparation for a higher position needs a different approach from one who is being coached in order to raise productivity. It also needs to be different from a person being coached in preparation for a transfer to an area with a different culture.

Disclose pertinent issues

If, for example, the department has been experiencing internal conflict, it is best to let the coach be aware. It may sometimes even be a situation of an expanding workforce where the old personnel seems to be overshadowed. That information is crucial because therein might lie issues of mistrust. And with that inside information, the coach will be able to tailor his or her approach to suit the situation.

Disclose any improvement steps taken

If the coaching is meant to straighten some rough patches, the coach needs to be aware of any other actions that have been taken before; including the specific period, they took place. Even the administrative steps fall into this scope. However, it is essential to appreciate that just because coaching is taking place does not relieve the supervisors or managers of their supervisory roles.

How do the employee and immediate supervisor get along?

The coach needs to know the kind of relationship that exists between the individual employees and their supervisors. If it is strained the coach will tailor the coaching in a way that will address the situation. Likewise, if it is too close, the coach will make a point of discussing it also so that the employee can take the supervisor's role with the seriousness it deserves.

How much does the employee know about the coaching?

It is imperative that you let the coach know what the employee has been told about the coaching. When you see the employee's perspective and expectations, then the journey to success is set as you will be working along the same lines.

Get the employee ready

Inform the employee of the coaching in advance

It is advisable that you let your employee know there is a coach set to call on them and work with them. And it is at that juncture that you explain why the coaching sessions are deemed necessary. Let the employee also feel that their voice can be heard regarding the timing as well as the venue.

The point here is that you need to avoid a scenario where the employee feels hijacked or even like a victim of a conspiracy. And that is precisely what would happen if the first time the employee hears about the coaching is in the presence of the coach; probably when the sessions are beginning.

Do not make a coaching session an additional meeting

You need to let your employee know the specific expectations for the coaching. For instance, spell out, in case the coaching is at the proposal stage, that you expect a fast response about how interested the employee is. Also, make it known that you expect the employee to adhere to agreed schedules without unnecessary lateness and cancellations. It is also essential that the employee participates actively by asking questions and being receptive to feedback.

What is the coaching set to achieve?
It is essential to have clear goals

Once goals are clear, both the coach and the employee can tell when they have made headway. Management too can understand.

Let the goals be the same for all parties

Having management set goals that are different from those of the employee cannot be right for the organization. This issue needs to be discussed. If, for instance, it is a case of the employee preparing to take up a new role, it is essential that his or her expectations be

15

those of the management; and where they differ, they need to discuss and find common ground.

The coach should identify needs

Usually, a coach helps to streamline issues of employee behavior in the prevailing circumstances. However, in the process of coaching, specific questions may be revealed that only management can address. For instance, you may have an excellent employee who, despite being devoted to the company, feels disadvantaged by the organization's remuneration structure. That is something that the coach may advise management upon.

The coach needs the ear of senior management

For coaching to yield the desired results, any deep-seated issues the employee has and which may inhibit the proper progress of the coaching need to be reported to senior management; that is, above the employee's immediate supervisor or manager. Discussing such details with the immediate supervisor or manager would be tantamount to breaching confidentiality, and that would even make the employee lose trust in the coach.

Coaching is not magic

Coaching is not like instant coffee that produces a beverage instantly. With coaching, all parties need to be aware that results can only show after a while. And so management should not begin getting anxious about not seeing an instant change from the employees involved. Preferably, it is essential that they be patient and they also render all the support possible so that the coached employees can find a supportive environment to implement what they learned from the coaching.

How far should confidentiality go?

Coach needs to keep the employees' information confidential

It needs to be spelled out from the beginning that all matters the employee discloses in conversation with the coach are to be treated as confidential by the coach. That makes the employee free to open up and volunteer information that can prove useful to the coaching process.

Confidentiality does not restrict the employee

As for the employee, there is freedom to share whatever is discussed or learned from the coaching sessions with any person they choose, including top management. On the other hand, they are not obligated to explain it either.

Feedback to supervisors or managers need to be general

Even as feedback is expected after every assignment, from the coach to the seniors of the employee, it should be presented in general terms. For instance, it needs to be regarding whether the employee adhered to schedules; was an active participant; was receptive; and so on. The details of what transpired are not to be disclosed.

There needs to be an exception clause for confidentiality

There are cases where the coach may feel the necessity to disclose information gained in the course of coaching like if there is a risk of someone getting injured or in there is concealed ongoing abuse in the workplace. To cater for such circumstances, the coach needs to be officially protected in his or her terms of engagement.

Spell out when the coach can terminate the contract prematurely

The situations where the coach is mandated to disclose acquired information is mentioned earlier is when the client is at risk of harm or other people are. How about if the client is involved in behavior that happens to be unacceptable in the coach's opinion? Confidentiality must still be maintained. However, the coach could encourage the employee to do the disclosing personally. Otherwise, the coach brings the sessions to a halt. The coach can give the employee an ultimatum for this.

The coaching goals should suit all group members

Although coaching is not an information dissemination program, you need to have people with a common purpose just like a class. The group members may, for instance, belong to the same department; be a group of people set to take up managerial positions soon; be people set to work on a typical project; and so on.

In group coaching, the coach needs to focus primarily on what affects the group and not the individual. If the individual's behavior or approach is to be addressed, it should be only as far as it has an impact on the success of the group.

It needs to be mentioned, however, that the individuals in the group need to be guided on how to make the best use of their talents and skills because in the process the overall group benefits; and the group fulfills its goals more efficiently.

A coach is set to succeed despite changing circumstances

A coach needs to be prepared for challenges

A good coach is not expected to take a template with him or her for the employees to complete. It is the coach to adjust to the client's environment and help out within the prevailing circumstances. So, if a coach finds an unexpected situation, it is up to him or her to adjust accordingly.

A coach needs to exercise patience

Whereas the guidance of a coach can begin to produce positive results within a short time, the real impact is usually felt long after the coaching sessions are done. That is something that the employee concerned, the management and the coach need to understand.

Chapter 3: What Is the Importance of Coaching?

Oh, how many times have you woken up feeling like you would not, if only you had a choice? So you go to the office just because you are not ready to lose your job, or you attend a sports training session only because you do not want to risk being chucked from the team when you miss the training. So, many are the times you keep to the straight path only because you have an overseer. But would you not enjoy a situation where you were excited to jump out of bed and get on with business? This is one of the things that a coach tries to do: get you to a place where you feel motivated to work or do whatever it is you have chosen to do.

And if you love something, why would you need someone else to push you?

No – a coach does not push you; at least not in the sense of forcing. The thing is – some challenges come your way even when you did not sign for them. Consider this:

You are trying to do your best in school basketball with the hope of being identified for NBA. Apart from one or two of your friends, and of course, your ever loyal mum, everyone else can only enumerate how many 6-footers never made it beyond college basketball, and how marginal your chances are of joining any top team. That is called discouragement and negative vibe.

Hopes are what they are. And so, for example, if you are hoping to join the NBA someday, you still cannot afford to slacken on your studies, for you know not if this basketball dream will come true. What would happen if you never got to join the league? You would need to have professional papers to make it in life.

Now, this is where the pressure comes in. No parent sends their kid to school to play basketball, soccer or whatever else. They send them to do academics, and the rest is just but incidental. And the pressure to maintain good academic grades and keep up your sports practice can be overwhelming.

Just because you have joined a sports team does not uproot you from the society. So things that are happening in the community around you get to you and have an impact on your mood, your attitude, and even your level of motivation. If, for instance, you have a brother who is vying for a political seat, and then either on TV or social media you see reports of how someone had thrown rotten eggs his way, it would get you off focus. And right there I can almost hear your breathing as you expend masses of negative energy.

The coach's role:

When such distractions occur, your coach helps you to downplay them. Not assuming they do not exist – no; just ensuring that you deal with them in a way that does not adversely affect your chosen pursuit.

A coach helps you to direct your thoughts to the goal that matters most at the time; keeping you least distracted.

A coach helps you to channel your energy to your chosen cause. For example, if you keep paying attention to opposing fans and responding to them, you will not have enough power to improve your act.

A coach helps you to remain focused. If you have a politician brother, for example, the coach makes you appreciate the need to chart your success path as opposed to being absorbed in your brother's fame. You get to hear the hard reality that even if you were to twist your leg on the court, your politician brother would not resign from Congress, Senate or whatever another office he may be holding. Likewise, you should not miss your training session just because the politicians are playing dirty in their arena.

In short, you get to learn that some negatives come with every territory and that it is okay to let those in the kitchen deal with the heat while you do what you have got to do. In summary, this is what you discuss and agree on with your coach:

What do you want to achieve?

What obstacles are you encountering or envisaging?

What action do you need to take to decimate those obstacles and pave the way for your success?

In general, coaching is about making inquiries into your perception, abilities, commitment, and challenges, and leading you to reflect on the whole situation. And in interrogating the status of the person you are coaching, you need to frame your questions in specific ways to be able to receive answers that are relevant and useful.

We shall, therefore, discuss different kinds of questions because sometimes you want to get the person opening up openly, and other times you want to, more or less, direct the person's line of thought. Of course, you appreciate that a question is not merely a question. There are those that you throw in the air to keep the conversation going. Think of the rhetorical questions, for example: *How could you have retained him as a manager anyway?* Here, you are not expecting your trainee to give you any answers because what you imply with that question is that nobody would have expected you to retain the person in question as your manager.

On the contrary, there are those questions that are geared towards extracting information from the person you are coaching. How you frame such questions matters; and how you follow up their answers also matters. And that is why it is essential that you pay keen attention to your trainee's verbal response and body language too.

Chapter 4: Qualities of a Good Coach

Who is a good coach? You can say that a good coach is one who can make his or her clients succeed. The question is what is it that the coach does to make the client successful? Besides knowing how to frame issues to extract much-needed information from the client, what else is required?

First of all, it is good to be practical and acknowledge that most organizations do not have a budget for external coaching. Many are those that leave the coaching to respective department managers who are assumed to have something helpful to impart to their juniors. The problem here is that coaching is not necessarily mentoring. And as already mentioned it is not tutoring either. It is, therefore, essential that those managers bestowed upon the role of coaching know precisely what is expected of them in this regard.

An Executive Coaching Survey done in 2010 indicated that 63% of significant organizations rely on internal coaching. And even amongst those, about half of them invest barely 10% or less of their time in coaching. Maybe coaching could be taken more seriously if it was clear what it aims to achieve.

How coaching helps:

It raises the employee's level of effectiveness at work

If every employee were to be effective, would that not define the organization's success? After all, the success of an entity is the total of the success of all departments under which employees work.

It gets the employee to think more broadly

This means that the employee will be able to link his or her input to the organization's overall success. This is different from when an employee sees his or her duties as isolated chores to be accomplished day by day or month by month. Again, it is in this broad way of thinking that an employee learns to improvise when specific resources are not available and adjust when things do not run as preset.

It recognizes an employee's strengths

How many employees are paid but underutilized just because of some organizational protocol or just because nobody realizes what a resource the person is? Such talent can be identified for more appropriate roles. While making the employee more comfortable, such a move would also be geared towards benefiting the organization more.

Coaching brings out any need there is for development

There are times you have a good employee who would be invaluable to the company if only they were better trained or better orientated. Whatever is the case, it can be discovered during coaching.

Setting challenging targets

Coaching is a two-way experience, and both the manager in charge of coaching and the employee being coached can settle on target goals during the coaching process. This would be fine because they have room to discuss what the hindrance would be and how to tackle them, and also what resources would be required to make them attain their goal.

At the end of the coaching process, the coach should be satisfied that he or she is leaving behind a person who is growing. The fact that the employee can think critically and be ready to make decisions that they can stand by is an indication of successful coaching.

Research from the Center for Creative Leadership has summed up the skills managers need to play marvelous coaches, and they are:

Managing to earn much-needed trust as well as respect from employees

To have the employees trust you, it is imperative that you set your boundaries as their senior and also to keep your promises. You surely cannot be the guy who staggers home in drunkenness from the same pub your employees frequent and expect to maintain acceptable boundaries.

What happens when they have to drag you to your car all lost and unruly? And what happens when you promise study leave that you have not even agreed with top management and then it does not get authorized? In short, for your employees to benefit from your coaching endeavors, you need to build a relationship of mutual respect and trust.

Ability to make a measurable assessment

The manager should be able to provide objective feedback on what the employee is missing out to reach the required level of performance and then discuss with the employee possible steps to be taken to amend that. After a reasonable duration, the manager should be able to make another assessment so that the employee can know how his or her efforts have impacted performance. In short, the following questions should acquire answers within reasonable timelines:

What were you unable to achieve as an employee and you are now making it?

What did you promise to do and you implemented it?

What were your intentions and were they realized?

Ability to get employees thinking critically

Here what is meant is particularly the skill to ask open-ended questions. That means the employee has room to go beyond a yes or a no in response. The employee can engage his or her mind and give actual observation and deductions. On encouraging this kind of thinking, the coach also promotes decision making based on reasonable assessment of a situation – and that includes a level of risk-taking.

Being supportive

The coaching manager is expected to be open-minded as they listen to their employees, and be able to empathize with them. The trust they have earned should be enough to encourage the employees to ventilate without fearing that they will be judged adversely. Without a doubt, it is more accessible to assist someone makes progress when you know what their frustrations are than otherwise. And in this spirit of being supportive, the manager needs to acknowledge good work and achievement of goals.

Chapter 5: Common Coaching Challenges and How to Handle Them

Do you think coaching is something every employee will embrace? If you think about the many unvoiced complaints that employees have from feeling under-remunerated to being in the wrong job, you will see why they would shun any further engagement, without giving it a chance. How about where individuals voluntarily hire coaches – are there challenges? There are challenges because some people only hear that having a coach leads to success. However, they fail to understand that a coach is not a magician and cannot work alone. So there are myriad reasons that make a coach's job one big challenge.

Here are some of challenges:

Client not being committed

How can you get an athlete, for instance, to reduce his or her personal best time by, say, a minute or two, if they are not willing to maintain a regular rest schedule?

The client having a procrastinating tendency

If you agree that the client is to begin training at a specific date and then that changes without proper notice, and not once or twice, that is an ominous sign for a coach. It means the coach is dealing with an unpredictable client. How can the coach even be sure of consistency once the coaching begins? Often, it may just be a sign of the client developing cold feet not knowing what to expect.

Inability to communicate effectively

A client who cannot speak out sincerely and without fear makes it difficult for the coach to decipher the weaknesses that need to be addressed. It follows then that improvement takes time and the client, in turn, begins to feel exasperated. Now, with both coach and the client handling frustrated, what success can this coaching engagement produce?

A client has no clue about coaching

When someone identifies natural talent and remarks that if you had a coach, you would do marvelous, this is not enough for you to be the best unless you first all charter a way forward. You need to know where you stand amongst other competitors, what you have achieved so far and where you need to be within a specified period. And this is what you need to let your coach know. With that knowledge then, you can have an idea the point at which you are starting and the position you would like to reach. With specific direction, the coach will find it easy to assist.

Some clients are not proactive

As mentioned before, some clients think that coaches come with an instant solution. It then becomes a significant challenge to get the client do his or her part with that kind of mentality. Nobody ever got to make them understand that no success comes without effort.

However, as long as the coach can anticipate challenges of this nature, they will be able to think ahead of ways to counter them and get the client succeeding despite a bumpy beginning.

Here are ways out for coaches:

As a coach, lay out a vivid picture of the outcome

Once the client can see the enviable image of success, they are likely to push excuses aside and focus on attaining the goal. It is a great way of motivating the client though it looks more like bait.

Have tiny goals first

It is understandable that one should be scared of how high a target is, especially if it is nothing close to where they are at the moment. The solution, however, is to break down the long-term goal into small goals that are achievable within a relatively short time. As a coach, you should be able to spell out the achievements to look out for after such a brief spell. The gratifying news, however, is that success, irrespective of how tiny it may appear, is motivating to the performer. In any case, succeeding in many successive small steps is the sure way of accomplishing the bigger goal.

Apply your communication techniques

The coach needs to apply all the communication techniques he knows to get the client to open up. This is where the personality of the coach comes in because a good one will be able even to alter his style to suit the personality of the particular client. He could, for instance:

Request for client's feedback at regular intervals

Adopt the communication style where you keep paraphrasing what you deem as what your client means, and of course ask the client to confirm that.

Volunteer exciting ideas and see if any of them stimulates your client into communicating more

Keep giving opinions and insights to try and provoke your client into participating

Inquire into vocational skills that your client has

Inquire into what makes your client tick

At the end of the day, you will be able, as a coach, to assist your client come up with a Purpose Statement, so that both of you know where you stand and where you are headed.

Chapter 6: Tips for Coaches

Can a good student succeed if the teacher's style is wanting? No – the main reason this particular guide is laying out some tips that are helpful to coaches of all calibers.

Guiding Principles for Coaches

A coach should have the spirit for the job

You will find it difficult to succeed as a coach if you take it strictly as an hourly job that you cannot touch before or after hours. If you have noticed, many great coaches have a parental or brotherly spirit. They mind what their clients are up to in every sphere of life. That not only creates a bond of respect but also makes the client feel accountable, a significant ingredient for success. And in this spirit of minding the welfare of the client as a whole, the coach avails himself or herself, at least by wireless, for support and encouragement, and also for quick unscheduled consultation.

Believing in a client's *ability* to unleash hidden potential

In other words, you are not a good coach just because you can refine a client who is already well performing, but because you can change the attitude of an ordinary client to a positive one and have him or her motivated enough to bring out talent not known before.

Getting satisfaction from helping others succeed

The spirit of giving and sacrificing for the sake of the client is necessary. As such, the coach cannot watch as the client falls off track only to point out the indiscipline or other weakness later. Instead, he or she tries to ascertain the client succeeds whatever the challenges.

Bringing out the client's best and allowing them to take lead

This essentially means that the coach is showing his or her trust in your abilities, which in turn boosts your self-confidence and encourages you to take the initiative. Similarly, when your coach observes this principle, as the client, you get accustomed to thinking of how to circumvent problems while tackling other challenges to the best of your ability. In due course, that atmosphere makes you develop a reasonable level of independence, which is what the coach would want for you ultimately.

Trying to influence the client rather than push and dictate

The relationship between a coach and the client needs to be friendly and not just one of respect. And that can only happen if the client feels valued and respected regarding having his or her opinions heard. Lack of such mutual understanding can lead to a strained relationship which is doomed to yield very little regarding coaching success.

Thriving on challenges and ability to adjust

A coach needs to be flexible and adaptable to circumstances affecting the client. Supposing the client had a part-time job but has now acquired a full-time job – is the coach going to freeze and begin to look for the exit clause in the contract? On the contrary, the coach would be expected to work out a convenient schedule with the client under the new circumstances.

Continuous self-development

You are going to remain a great coach who is confident of his or her efficiency in delivering results if only you keep learning and improving your skills. There are seminars and workshops; newsletters; and also other coaches that you can rely on to better yourself and keep yourself challenged. In the process, you can keep your skills sharpened and love for your job enhanced.

How to Build a Relaxed Relationship of Trust

As already mentioned here before, trust between the coach and the client is vital if the coaching process is to be successful. Communication also needs to be comfortable and not strained. How do you cultivate that atmosphere as a coach?

By maintaining sincere communication that builds rapport between the two of you

By having a good sense of humor

By being sincere in your caring for the client

By practicing integrity in the way you handle your client and his or her affairs

Why You Should Mind Your Questions as a Coach

Are we saying that some inquiries are out of bounds? No, not inquiries, but the manner of making them. It is understandable that you should ask your client questions. In fact, asking questions is encouraged because it is only after extracting information that the client had not volunteered before that you can know how to proceed with your coaching.

Ask questions that excite your client in a right way and those that are likely to leave you both inspired

Ask questions that make the client feel empowered and valued

Shelve any questions that you think may come across as judgmental

Avoid problems that ultimately sound like a roundabout way of dishing out advice

Go for great items as they are geared towards eliciting deep thinking and great answers or solutions. Of course, such questions reflect curiosity in an explicit manner.

Your questions need to reflect empathy for your client's situation as much as they are meant to show curiosity.

Make good use of your intuition

One reason you are considered a good coach is that you know how to make a sound judgment. So in this regard:

Know when to listen attentively to your client without offering advice

Train yourself always to be present when communicating with your client. Your client can tell when you are half attentive and it does not do any good to your relationship

Suppress the temptation to jump to conclusions prematurely

Have an open mind. It helps keep biases and prejudices out of your work

Use your intuition to decide what to say and when to say it.

Chapter 7: The responsibilities of a coach

A wise person once said that coaches, no matter the field of activity, are instrumental in helping other people. The truth is that coaching often goes beyond giving advice, with the coach working hard to achieve some specific objectives in a short period.

At first glance, coaching might seem like a simple matter. However, when you take a closer look, you will see that a lot of effort is put into helping other people. A coach has to take on some responsibilities, having a limited timeframe in which he/she can help other people. Specific objectives to be reached must be identified, as well as the best strategies to pursue them.

Responsibilities to yourself as a coach

Often, as a coach, you guide people who are confused, not knowing what step to take next, with regarding their personal or professional lives. If you are equally confused, how can you be of help?

So, you see, there are some responsibilities, which you must consider about yourself. You need to lead an organized existence, to be able to coach others into reaching the same level of success. Just think about it. Let's say that a person comes to you, asking for help, in becoming better organized around the workplace. If you are not organized yourself, you cannot hope to help another person make such a change. You have to work on yourself first.

Another considerable responsibility is related to the standards you have set for yourself. Professional coaches know that one must first set realistic expectations regarding themselves; once you are reasonable with the things you expect from your own life, you will find it easier to work with other people and help them progress. On the other hand, if you have set standards that are too high to reach, you stand a good chance to fail. It is evident that this will have a negative impact on the coaching process at the same time.

In short, when you think of yourself as a coach, you have to look at the bigger picture. You will be invited into another person's life and be given a chance to influence his/her present, as well as the future. Your vision has to go beyond the present moment, primarily when you evaluate the best strategies that can be followed.

Responsibilities you have towards the clients(s)

As a coach, you have some responsibilities towards your client(s), regardless of the field of activity. As it was already mentioned above, you need to set realistic expectations, starting with yourself and continuing with your client. Depending on his/her needs, you have to work on attaining the desired objectives, in a timeframe as short as it is possible. For this reason, you might be responsible for establishing some milestones that the client has to go through, until reaching the bigger, final goal. Moderation is the key here, so you may want to avoid setting goals that are hard or even impossible to reach. If you are expectations are unrealistic, your client might feel overwhelmed and quit before achieving anything.

Even though coaching is an entirely different process from the one of counseling, you might find yourself taking on the role of counselor, from time to time. Regular meetings with the client have to be established, to discuss the set milestones and how these can be best reached. The constant interaction with the coachee is one of the primary responsibilities to be assumed, especially since it will allow you to keep track of the progress made.

Whether you act as a personal or professional coach, you still have the massive responsibility of providing the coachee with the support he/she needs, to improve his/her personal/business life.

Even though the relationship between a coach and his/her coachee does not unravel on a long-term basis, this does not mean that it doesn't bear a great significance. An individual approach is preferred for every coachee, for the best strategies to be determined and followed.

From a pragmatic point of view, the coach has the responsibility of meeting with each client in particular. In these meetings, the coach and the coachee will discuss existent needs, desired goals and possible obstacles that have to be overcome. As the coaching continues, meetings will be held, to develop short-term strategies and register the progress made. Adjustments to the original plan will also be made, if necessary.

What does it mean to be a responsible coach?

A responsible coach is a person who presents both the knowledge and experience the client requires. Moreover, he/she is a person who is genuinely interested in helping other people, exhibiting a pure passion for the field(s) the client is active in. Personal traits make sure people better coaches than others, such as cheerfulness, encouragement, and optimism.

The truth is that a professional coach, one who shows both integrity and responsibility, will always put the client in the first place. Coaches need to be able to set personal matters aside and work in the interest of the client, first and foremost. Each coaching session requires an excellent clarity of mind, so you have to clear your head and focus on your client, and nothing else.

It might take some time before you learn to clear your head and avoid thinking about trivial things, but, in the end, you will see how beneficial this is. A clear head allows you to pay total and complete attention to your client, hearing his/her problems and providing the best strategies for these to be solved. When you put your client in the center of attention, every coaching session will be a complete success.

Chapter 8: Coaching tools and techniques

At first glance, you might be tempted to say that coaching is all about asking questions and challenging the coachee to come up with the best possible answers. However, for the coaching process to be successful, things have to be far more complicated. Professional coaches often resort to some coaching tools and techniques, to establish a relationship with their clients and help them achieve the desired objectives. In the paragraphs that follow, you will be able to discover some of these tools and techniques.

Wheel of life

The bike of life is pure to use, being highly efficient, especially when it comes to identifying the things that are weighing one down. It can also be used to determine future goals and the best strategies for these to be achieved.

Perhaps the most significant advantage of the wheel of life is that it offers a visual representation of both the current and the future situation. You can begin by drawing a circle, in which the client will add all of the essential elements in his/her life. Most people concentrate on their career, relationships, and health status but any other item can be added, as long as it bears an essential significance in that person's life.

Socratic Method

The Socratic Method is used in a wide array of fields, including as part of the coaching process, being based on the idea of asking questions and challenging the client to come up with the best answers to those questions. In coaching, this method can be adapted, to include some specific issues, related to your desired goals, current situation, available options and willpower presence (or lack thereof).

The main idea is that you, as a coach, use these questions to guide the client in the desired direction, helping him/her think positively. Once you have managed to change his/her pattern of thinking, you will find it easier to discuss potential outcomes and set future goals. Plus, you will no longer have difficulties in choosing goals that follow the SMART pattern.

Begin the discussion with the goals your client envisioned. Are these meant for a short or long-term basis? In how much time will those goals be achieved? Discuss how realistic and feasible these goals are, as well as about the tools that can be used to measure them. Last, but not least, ask a fundamental question: why did you choose these goals in particular?

After you have covered these goals, move on to the present situation. You need to make your client aware of the current case, of the things that are alright and the things that are weighing him/her down. The client must be forced to look at the big picture and understand that it is not possible to achieve the set goals all at once; on the contrary, one has to go through some smaller steps, for success to be possible.

Get into details and discuss the options the client has. Is it possible to go in an alternative direction? What are the positive and negative points of each of the available options? Does the pressure of time force your client to go down a particular road? You need to be straight with your client and get things out. Otherwise, the coaching process will not succeed.

You are also responsible for bringing his/her willpower into the limelight. Talk about the things that have to be done first, the obstacles that can appear along the way and how these can be overcome. Also, ask your client whether additional help or financial/non-financial support would change his/her perspective on the matter.

Human body & emotions

Many people fail to achieve the goals they have set for themselves, because they are unable to correctly identify their own feelings. Using this exercise, you can help your client understand how to identify various emotions and use them to his/her advantage.

What you want to do is take two sheets of paper and draw a human body on each. You do not have to put a lot of effort into it but make sure your drawing does resemble a human body. At the top of each of the two human bodies, place a positive, respectively, negative emotion. Then, ask the client to remember and provide details for an actual event/situation, which led to the feeling in question. Go into more information and ask the client to remember how the excitement felt like. The more you engage in this exercise, the easier it will become for the client to identify his/her own feelings.

Animal association

We all associate ourselves with an animal, whether consciously or unconsciously. This association can provide a lot of valuable information on who we are and how we perceive ourselves. Prepare your client by telling him/her you are going to ask some questions, to which you are expecting an immediate answer (these are usually provided by the unconscious mind, which means they are not controlled but somewhat spontaneous and natural).

The first question that you want to ask your client is what kind of animal does he/she associate himself/herself with. Then, discuss about the reasons for which he/she has chosen that particular animal in the first place. Do not stop here and ask your client about how that animal represents he/she. T

Old & young

Ever since we are little, we are taught that each of us, as an individual, possess some strengths and qualities.

This is an excellent exercise, as it allows one to identify how much he/she has progressed. The client will see that he/she has accumulated a lot of experience, knowledge, and skills, which are highly useful in the present. Ask your client to concentrate only on the positive things and how his/her life has changed for the better. Once he/she is aware of these positive things, it will be easier to focus on future goals and the best ways to achieve them.

Chapter 9: Code of ethics

Potter Stewart: "Ethics is knowing the difference between what you have a right to do and what is right to do."

Both coaches and mentors are required to follow a global code of ethics, established by the European Mentoring & Coaching Council. The main idea behind this code of ethics is to ensure the best practices in the field of coaching, as well as of mentoring. Once the best practices are maintained and promoted, one can talk about excellence in the respective areas.

The Global Code of Ethics for Coaches and Mentors was established with the purpose of developing a set of standards for the people who are active in this field. It regulates the behavior when working with different clients, ensuring an organized framework for professional growth and development. The code is divided into four sections, every section guiding the expression of a professional coach while establishing some rules to follow for the best possible conduct. These sections are terminology, working with clients, professional, and excellent practice.

Terminology

This section of the code of ethics regards your designation as a coach/mentor, as well as the responsibilities and duties attached to the chosen profession.

Working with clients

This is an essential section of the ethics code, containing some essential elements, to be remembered and respected. As a coach, you are responsible for taking all necessary measures to understand the expectations of the client and how these should be met.

You are committing to abide by the guidelines established in this code, being open to your clients about any methods, tools or techniques that you might use.

Integrity

You are bound as a professional coach to demonstrate integrity in work with all clients, representing your qualifications in a relevant manner. At the same time, any ideas that you present to your client, have to be attributed to the person who was responsible for them in the first place (claiming them as your own is not only unethical but also illegal).

Confidentiality

It is clear that the relationship between the coach and the coachee is confidential but, sometimes, it is possible to forget that information should not be released to third parties. The only exception to this rule is if law requires the information release. You are also responsible for storing all the information connected to the client safely and securely, even after the coaching process has ended. In the situation that the client has undertaken illegal activities or is at risk of harming himself or others, you are free from the confidentiality rule. However, you will be required to inform the client that you are no longer maintaining confidentiality.

Inappropriate interactions

First and foremost, you are bound to treat all clients the same, regardless of their race, gender or skin color. As a coach, you need to demonstrate cultural sensitivity and avoid racial, ethnic or cultural stereotypes. At the same time, you are forbidden from engaging in relationships with your client, whether these are of a romantic or sexual nature.

Conflict of interest

The relationship between the coach and the coachee is based on mutual trust and, you, as a coach, should never try to take advantage of this relationship. You are bound to avoid any conflict of interest and, if such a dispute arises, you should immediately inform the client. The next step would be to end the coaching agreement and recommend another suitable coach to your client.

Termination of professional relationships

The client can terminate the coaching engagement at any point he/she desires, while you, as a coach, have to respect his/her wishes. If the coaching process does not provide the desired results, you should not continue the engagement but rather withdraw from the relationship and recommend a compatible coach. It is also essential to remember that you have responsibilities towards your client, even after the completion of the coaching engagement. These responsibilities are mostly related to confidentiality and the safe storage of client data.

Professional conduct

This section helps you to maintain excellent standards in your work with different clients, ensuring the best practices for the coaching industry. By adhering to the rules of professional conduct, you will no doubt behave respectfully, recognizing the importance of equality and diversity. The section also covers the breaches regarding professional conduct, as well as the obligation and duties of both coaches and mentors.

Excellent practice

This section covers the qualifications that are necessary for practicing as a coach, as well as the health standards that one must fulfill. You will also find information on the on-going supervision regarding your work as a coach, not to mention the importance of pursuing continuous professional development.

Chapter 10: Coaching myths debunked

The coaching profession is rarely understood for what it is and there are a lot of people who transmit this false information further on to others. In this chapter, we will present some of the most famous coaching myths, as well as the truth behind them.

Myth 1: Coaching demands an extended period to succeed

As it was already mentioned above, coaching is meant to be undertaken for short periods of time. However, even if it extends beyond the usual period, you have to understand that it is an investment in yourself. In general, for the coaching process to succeed and one to achieve his/her objectives, it is enough to visit your coach for a two-hour session, for several weeks in a row. Or, if you prefer, you can see your coach at rarer periods of time, making sure to track your progress regarding the professional development nevertheless.

Myth 2: Coaching is not meant for people who are successful, but rather for those who have problems

This is one of the most common myths associated with coaching, with many people who are facing financial difficulties or problems turning to a professional coach as a last-minute, desperate solution. In reality, coaching works best with people who are motivated, having already reached a point of success in their lives. It helps them increase their overall performance and escape the sensation of feeling stuck so that they can move on to the next level.

Successful people benefit the most from coaching, especially when they have some challenges that they want to overcome or essential objectives to be reached. It is often recommended for leaders who are preparing to assume new positions within individual organizations, with added responsibility and pressure. However, when it comes to saving people from their problems, it rarely works. This is because, most of the times, such people are not interested in the help a coach will provide. Their poor performance is associated with a lack of motivation, not to mention they will resist any suggestions coming from the outside. So, you see, it is successful and motivated people who instead guarantee a good return on an investment such as the one of coaching.

Myth 3: Coaching is the same thing with mentoring

We have already discussed the differences between coaching and mentoring, but we are going to review this in this short paragraph. A mentor has a different work cut out for him/her, in comparison to the coach. He/she will establish a more informal relationship with the mentoree, being set on providing general counseling and advice on how certain things can be achieved or changed. A coach, on the other hand, will work on specific goals with the coachee, establishing a time limit for the achieving of those objectives and making sure that a relationship of mutual trust has also been established.

Coaching should never be confused with mentoring, as these are two distinct processes of human development. The most important thing that you have to remember is that a coach will never tell you what to do, as opposed to a mentor, who might assume this role from time to time. The coach will work with you, so that you develop your inner strength and find the answers to the questions you might have, by yourself.

Myth 4: Only people in a leading position can benefit from coaching

We often hear about senior managers or executives working for a dominant company resorting to coaching, to improve their overall performance and achieve specific objectives. However, in reality, these are not the only kind of people who can benefit from coaching.

Originally, coaching engagements have been designed for people who occupied leading positions and demonstrated a lot of potentials. Nevertheless, today, coaching is recommended for a wide range of professionals and specialists, including those who are in mid-level positions. It is often used for people who have been promoted, to get them up to speed with what happens in the respective organization or the new position. So, you see, managers of all levels, including mid-level executives, can derive tremendous benefits from a coaching engagement.

Myth 5: Coaching will require a lot of money, as it is costly

Before you decide that coaching is too expensive for you, take a moment and compare it with other opportunities for personal/professional development. Just think about the costs associated with a training seminar or a leadership development program. You have to cover the costs of traveling, find suitable accommodations and pay for them. The overall cost also entails three meals a day, the training fees and, not to mention, you will lose some money, by being away from work.

By comparison, the coaching engagement is much more affordable, as it only requires a minimum of two hours per week, for several weeks. There are no costs related to traveling, as the coaching process is undertaken locally, no additional fees to be paid and you will still have time to go to work. What more could you wish for? So, the next time you will say no to coaching, thinking that it is too expensive for your budget, think again.

Chapter 11: How to be a competent coach

Coaching, when successful, improves a person's performance, playing an essential role in helping the person in question reach a new point in his/her life. In the past few years, more and more people have turned their attention towards coaching, understanding how important it is. However, not all coaching engagements prove out to be successful... which leaves us wondering: what does it take for the coaching process to be active?

It all starts with answering two fundamental questions: "why does that person need coaching" and "what actions must I take as a coach, to help that person succeed." As a coach, your sole focus in on helping another person discover the best ways, in which he/she can develop and grow.

Step 1: Establish a relationship of mutual trust

If you want your coachee to listen to your advice and learn from your experience/knowledge, you need to work hard and establish a relationship of mutual trust.

When you are clear about the direction of the learning process and the objectives you consider that is needed to be achieved, the coachee will find it easier to accept you as his/her coach. As a coach, you are responsible for demonstrating good judgment and be patient with your coachee, until the desired objectives are reached. You also need to work with him/her, so as to make sure that he/she does not quit and fights for some specific goals.

Step 2: Track the progress of your coachee

At the beginning of the coaching engagement, you will analyze the situation of the coachee and come with the best strategies to achieve some specific objectives. You will take your coachee, from where he/she is in the present, to where he/she does want to go.

You will continuously work with this person, helping him/her gain self-awareness and become more confident. Apart from that, you will have to provide him/her with constant feedback, for every milestone that was achieved. The feedback given to the coachee can be of tremendous help, especially if the client is willing to make a change in his/her professional behavior or conduct.

In tracking the progress made by the coachee, you will have to provide a fair assessment, making sure to point out any mistakes one has made. A permanent comparison will be made between the current and desired performance, not to mention you will have to work on helping the client go from words to action. For the coaching process to be active, it is essential to go over the intention phase and work to make an actual impact on that person's future.

Step 3: Challenge your coachee to think

A good coach does not force feed his/her coachee with suggestions, forcing him/her to go in a particular direction. Instead, he/she challenges his/her coachee to think and come up with the best answers to the questions he/she has. To be an effective coach, you will have to ask a lot of open-ended questions, leaving your client to think for himself/herself.

By challenging your coachee to think, you will have the pleasant surprise to see him/her coming up with efficient solutions to his/her problems. You will instill the necessary confidence, encouraging him/her to take risks and face existent challenges.

Step 4: Provide support and encouragement

You and your coachee are partners, going together down the same road. You go through the learning process along, but you have the responsibility of guiding this process. The coachee might have a hard time working to achieve his/her objectives, feeling tempted to quit and withdraw from the coaching engagement. In such situations, it is your responsibility to provide the necessary support and encouragement.

You have to listen to your coachee, be open to his/her suggestions and try to allow for a healthy expression of one's emotions, without passing judgment. Coaches encourage their clients to work hard and celebrate each achieved milestone, welcoming the progress one has made. They recognize the achievement of the set objectives, withdrawing with respect from the coaching engagement.

Step 5: Work for actual results

You cannot begin a coaching engagement, without thinking about the goals or objectives that you want to achieve. If you're going to be a competent coach, you have to help the coachee come up with goals that bear meaning. You can also work with him/her, to identify the changes that need to be made to the present behavior and conduct.

Active coaches work for actual results, whether these regard small milestones or a larger goal to be achieved. The coach helps with the clarification of each milestone, as well as with the measurement of the progress made. Periodical assessments are required, to track the progress made and quantify the results obtained in the said period.

Chapter12: Effective Questions For A Coaching Model

Coaching is going to require that you ask many questions, the skill is to do so in a way that it does not come across as an interrogation. Generally speaking, there are three types of questions that you will find useful, and we will cover each of these in detail in this chapter:

Curious Questions

Clarifying Questions

Possibility Questions

With an arsenal of these questions at your disposal, you will find that getting the information and responses that you require from those you are mentoring will be a lot easier. The primary key to understanding these questions right is to phrase them in a non-judgmental way, a way that is going to build the relationship and trust rather than destroy it. For example, "Why did you let the whole team down?" is a question that is bound to elicit a defensive response because it seems accusatory. A better approach would be, "What went wrong on the project?"

Curious Questions

When it comes to strange questions, you need to be particularly careful in their phrasing, or they may come off as accusatory. Strange questions start off with the following:

How?

What?

Why?

When?

Supposing?

Curious questions should always be:

Short and sweet – keep it to a maximum of 10 words.

Concisely stated – Within the word count allowed, to ensure that you make it clear what you want to be answered.

No "Yes" or "No" answers – leave the question open-ended to allow your mentee to expand upon their response and explain their reasons more fully. This will help you to empathize with them better. You may also find that looking at things from a whole new angle sheds fascinating light on the situation.

Now that you know the essentials of what your curious questions should be, it is time to talk a little on the phrasing of the problems.

As mentioned above, the last thing that you want to do is to put the person on the defensive so do take some time to compose the questions before you set them. If your mentee is on the defensive, they will keep looking for ways to justify their actions/ answers, and this will not help anyone come to a better solution.

For example, "Why are you always so late getting to work?" is going to put your employee on the defensive immediately. On the other hand, you could say, "What reasons would you attribute to a delay in getting to work?" In both cases, you are asking the same thing but the second question is a softer approach.

Think about the question before you ask it and view it from your employees point of view – how would you react if you were them? Be creative when phrasing your questions.

During the conversation that ensues, empathetic listening comes into play. Pick up on a phrase or two in the answers and build upon that in the next question. That way, you get more of the information that you want without coming across as an inquisitor.

Do set this session at a time when you have enough time to devote to it. You must ask no more than one question at a time and be able to consider the responses given and your answers as well.

Also, be careful that you do not go into too much detail explaining your question or give hints as to what answers you were hoping to get – you want honest answers, not what the mentee is hoping you want to hear.

Also be careful about how you react to the answers given – even when you don't agree with them. If you get defensive when issues are brought up, your mentee will no longer feel comfortable raising concerns with you. If on the other hand, you demonstrate some empathy, your mentee will be encouraged to grow more questions, allowing you to get to the heart of the problem.

Clarifying Questions

It would be great if we could ask the right curious questions and get all our answers that way. Unfortunately, in the real world, it just does not work that way. There are going to be times when you will need more details – where perhaps the mentee has not explained themselves, or you do not fully understand the answer or where you need them to provide more information. For these times, clarifying questions are vital.

The aim here is to clarify what you have been told. For example, "Am I to understand that the bus service in your area is very unreliable?" You could also take this chance to ask more probing questions. For example, "Is it possible to find an alternate means to get to work?"

Again, the aim here is to ask questions that are more open-ended. By this stage in the conversation, however, you should have built up some trust so you can afford to be a little more direct. (While still taking care not to put the person on the defensive.)

Possibility Questions

If you want the mother-load of information, possibility questions are the best way to get it. The aim here is to get more information and perhaps to lead your mentee in the direction of coming up with a solution. For example, you could ask when training should start. By making them consider and give input on the possibilities, you automatically make it easier for them to buy into the solution as well because they helped to come up with it.

So yes, again here we want open-ended questions, but we do want to take a more targeted approach. Let's look at the problem, "When should training start?". While it is a valid question, it is not targeted enough – you could end up discussing the matter all day.

Now while your mentee could answer the possible questions posed to them, you can get a more targeted approach to steering the problem correctly. And by this, I mean giving some guidelines regarding the scope of the answer – not trying to make them give you the answer that you want.

The most useful aspect of possible questions is that they can encourage your mentee to come up with the solution on their own, seemingly without your interference. This can make a great deal of difference when it comes to being able to implement the solution as mentees will think it was their idea.

There are a couple of ways to drive the conversation – you could pose the question and give a few possible solutions, or you could raise the problem and provide the options of different answers.

For example, "Would you like to sign up now or do you want some time to talk to your family about it?"

When it comes to possible questions be guided by your mentee and what you know about them – if they are prone to over-analyze things, apply stricter targeting; if they are hard to draw into a conversation, use a looser rein.

Chapter13: Powerful coaching skills

Getting into the Right Mindset

Being a competent coach is all about having the appropriate mindset. The attitude you bring to this pursuit plays a role in every aspect of the experience of leadership, from how well team members listen to you, to be able to motivate them, to the level of respect they will show you when you express your authority.

Without the appropriate mental state for coaching, you will not be successful. People respond to what you put forth, even when it's nonverbal. This means being aware of the quality of your presence.

Coaching as a Tool for Growth

In many situations, people view the coaching practice as a means for correcting mistakes, to be used only when there's a problem. While this is a useful aspect of the method, coaching is a more positive experience all around when it's used not only as a corrective tool but as an approach for helping people to discover their strengths, identify their ambitions, and set about achieving them effectively.

Deciding on a training course and throwing it at your team members and hoping for the best outcome doesn't always work.

Being a coach with a growth perspective involves paying attention to each's strengths and bringing them out. It consists in being adaptable and listening. Although coaches are not gurus or counselors, many of them borrow methods from professionals in these fields.

Performance Coaching

Performance coaching suggests a new approach to management based on hands-on experience. You, the authority figure, are focusing on the objectives of the team, meaning that the results matter. Focusing too much on the result, however, can have a detrimental effect. It's all about the development of the full potential of your team, learning to identify and nurture each personality and strength. This involves staying receptive, aware, and innovative.

When you are coaching from a perspective of the ultimate goal, you lose sight of the experience of the journey. You stop seeing individuals, and you start seeing tasks. This disconnects you from the essence of the team and the people within it. Performance coaching requires that you pay attention to what is happening here and now and adjust your style and techniques accordingly.

Coaching Is About Unlocking Potential

For many managers, providing training is just another list item on their busy schedules, and they see team-member development as less important than the tasks they must achieve.

Not only will team goals be more easily accomplished, but it will be a smoother and happier experience for all parties involved and reduce friction and tension. A great leader knows how to create a positive and exciting environment while making sure that his team members stay on track and focused. He is the perfect balance between fun and business and understands that laughter is often an essential aspect of successful business or tasks of any kind.

The Importance of Having the Right Mindset as a Coach

As a coach or manager, it's important to remember that you are not just trying to instill something specific into someone to get better results. You are unlocking something that already exists within them. It's true that teaching, mentoring, and coaching all share qualities and specific necessary skills, but they are not the same thing, and it's important to understand how. Let's look at some of the critical differences between training, mentoring, and coaching.

Teaching /Training:

Teachers and trainers are given the task of imparting specialized knowledge to a student or students. In this way, education is similar to coaching. Although effective teachers are aware of interactive training methods and employ them regularly, there is an apparent imbalance of expertise in this dynamic.

The teacher is always assumed to have the right answers, while the student is just there to absorb the information, as opposed to a coaching relationship where the answers are discovered interactively.

Mentoring:

In mentoring, there is a consensus that the mentor is a guiding force who is there to show someone how to achieve things faster than they would on their own. In this way, it is similar to coaching.

Mentoring is different, however, in that the relationship typically focuses on future results, the development of one's career, and broadening horizons for the participant. Coaching tends to focus more on issues that are relevant to the present moment and finding ways to solve them.

Teaching and Mentoring vs. Coaching:

While a teacher or a mentor is viewed as an expert on the subject at hand, coaching focuses on equipping the individual to discover their unique potential. Rather than the material, the focus lies heavily on the person being coached and what is going on inside of them. A coach is not always someone specially designated; just about anyone can take this approach including peers or authority figures.

Instead of the sole focus being on imparting knowledge or skills to a person, the critical discussion of coaching lies in knowing how to ask the right questions to guide the individual through solving their issues.

Coaching Is About Helping People Solve Their Problems

One method employed by successful coaches is interactively teaching people to follow their instincts. It's not telling the person that you are the sole owner of the right solution and that they must blindly follow you. It's instead teaching them to get in touch with their potential and learn to get there themselves. Coaches equip people with this ability instead of asking them to submit. Some ways for a leader to help people solve their issues are:

Teaching them to silence their inner dialogue:

One way of bringing out these qualities is assisting the trainee in silence their inner voice. The body knows exactly what to do to achieve excellent performance; it's just a matter of freeing oneself from the distraction that internal dialogues can cause. To effectively help people solve their problems, removing fear and separating oneself from anxious self-talk is necessary. Once this barrier is removed, the coach can efficiently support the individual's learning process and consequently their overall performance.

Helping them identify specific goals:

To know where you're headed, you must be aware of your personal goals. A successful coach will help people recognize these if they aren't already aware of them. One way to do this is taking some time to think over goals and write them down. A coach can ask his team to think on this and write down three goals for the season and to check in on the status of the goals each week, reviewing and revising as time goes on. At the end of the season, the targets can then be considered again and given an assessment.

Helping them spot potential roadblocks:

To reach your full potential, you must be aware of potential obstacles to success. This means assessing yourself realistically, paying attention to the places you've fallen short in the past, and developing strategies for overcoming similar problems in the future. When a good coach notices a team member making a mistake, he knows the right questions to ask to call attention to this mistake and inspire creative solutions.

Without This Being Strong, You Are Just A Mean Boss

We've all had a mean boss; someone who cared more about numbers and getting things done than creating a harmonious environment in the workplace. Efficient coaches know how to avoid coming across this way. They are aware of the importance of building a healthy relationship between themselves and the person they are coaching.

Yelling orders at people and being too rigid is not the way to accomplish this. The relationship must be built on trust and mutual respect for it to be harmonious and healthy. Only then can the team member flourish and perform to their full potential.

Simple Ways to Enhance and Build the Person-and-Coach Relationship and Strengthen Respect

Logical leaders who are interested in the practical aspects of achieving goals understand the importance of improving upon and enhancing what already exists within the person being coached. They know that they must be there for the person they are leading. They are more than just a boss or supervisor. They are partners partaking in a relationship between coaches and coached, highly aware of the fact that the coaching dynamic depends upon interaction. The way they listen, take in and reflect upon questions, and provide feedback is all paid attention to and respected. Great coaches are aware of specific techniques that make them useful.

Listen Genuinely:

Partaking in good listening involves being curious about what you're hearing. Every valuable coach knows how to do this, and anyone who would like to become a valuable coach will learn. It's easy to get caught up in tasks and accomplishments and forget to listen with an attentive ear. This type of attitude comes across to the team member and creates discouragement. When a team member comes to you, make sure you're not the one doing all the talking. Be sure to try not to interrupt, while also keeping the topic focused.

Absorb What You Hear:

It's possible to go through the physical motions of listening and appear on the surface to be paying close attention to what the other person is saying. Even so, you may be too distracted to be absorbing any of it. In addition to seeming genuinely curious, don't neglect to make an effort to register what they are saying honestly. This is more than just listening to words; you must pick up on gestures, read emotions, and take in the ideas of the other person. This means setting the pace for the conversation and remembering to put yourself in their shoes.

Supplying Quality Feedback:

Feedback is a word that often has a negative connotation. It's thought of as criticism and nothing else. When employed the right way, however, it can have a very positive effect. Active coaches know how to go about providing feedback in a way that inspires. They don't use input as a way to assert their authority over the person but instead make sure it's entirely relevant and helpful. This makes it a favorable exchange.

Perhaps the most critical aspect of establishing a healthy coach-team member relationship is the knowledge of how to accurately reflect on the information they give you. In addition to the steps outlined above, a great coach should learn this skill to create the optimal dynamic.

The Secret to Finding Solutions

The ultimate key to finding great and appropriate solutions is the knowledge of how to ask the right questions.

You must be interactive with your conversations, as a coach. Asking the team member questions allows for a flow of back and forth information and more effective communication.

How Questioning Encourages Exploration:

Helps The Person Find Their Solution

Try to focus on open questions as opposed to simple "yes or no" questions. This will give them the chance to find their answers as well as provide them with practice for doing this in the future.

Showing them that they can find their solutions will be an empowering experience for the person. When you ask open questions, this indicates that you have faith in their ability to answer. It shows that you respect their opinion, which builds their confidence and performance.

Helps The Person Explore All Aspects of Their Problem

By asking simple "yes or no" questions, you aren't inviting the person talking to expand upon their ideas. You are shortening the conversation and closing doors for a potential learning experience. Asking thoughtful, open-ended questions will ensure that the team member can actively explore each angle of the issue at hand.

Questions Make You a Helper, Not a Boss

Unless you're interested in being a coach solely for the authority, it grants you, and you should ask thoughtful questions. Consider the concept of asking vs. telling. Merely giving orders to people puts across the idea that you are the one with all the answers and that they are your subordinate. In an active coaching relationship, the person being coached is an equal participant. This means you ask for their input. Asking questions and helping someone find a solution on their own allows you, as a coach, to be perceived as a helper.

Questions Help to Challenge the Old Thinking and Assumptions of the Person Being Coached

The beauty of conversations is being exposed to new perspectives you've never considered before. Instead of providing them with the answers, you're helping them identify and use their guidance system. This will show them that they are capable of being independent and innovative and increase their confidence.

The Forgotten Law of Getting Better Results

To effectively help team members reach their potential, you must hold them accountable. This means you've made yourself aware of what this person is capable of, and you are making sure they make it there.

Accountability gives the coach permission to help the person accomplish what they desire to achieve by being honest and straightforward in working towards a goal.

To Effectively Hold People Accountable, You Must

Decide on a Goal

Vague and general ideas of wanting to be better are not enough to reach full potential. This requires thought and particular intentions. Only once someone has pinpointed their goal can they effectively work toward achieving it. To accomplish things, we must first know what is worth performing, which means deciding on a specific purpose.

Be Clear On Expectations for Both the Coach and Person

The team cannot reach your expectations if they don't know what they are, just as you cannot perform your duties as a coach without knowing exactly what they entail. Clear communication is of utmost importance for a harmonious environment and optimal performance, both for you and the team.

Have Set Times to Check-In

Most teams have regular meeting times to review where they regard goals and what needs to be worked on. This not only keeps everyone on the same page and aware of the status of the situation at hand, but having specific times at which to check in and review will also push team members to excel beforehand. Designating times to check in could look like any of the following:

A pre-session or pre-practice meeting:

This can be a custom that you make a tradition. This meeting could keep fresh in each person's mind exactly what they need to be working on that day, as well as providing tips or advice as to how to achieve those goals.

Week discussions:

Instead of having a meeting before every practice, you can make sure you have one once a week.

Be Honest about Where the Person is by Asking Them Questions

Instead of making assumptions, effective leaders figure out where people are by asking. It's not fair to come at someone assuming that you already know exactly what's going on with them. Approaching the situation curiously and openly and discussing the answers is a better method. This will ensure that the person feels comfortable coming to you next time they have a problem, instead of keeping it to themselves. It also provides them with the ability to discover their answers and learn to believe in them.

Communication skills: This Skill Keeps Everyone on Track

Communication skills are of utmost importance in a harmonious coaching relationship. To help a person reach their full potential, you must know how to contact them. There are some critical questions you can ask yourself to make sure you're staying on track in this area.

Conclusion

Good coaching is a simple and cost-effective way to zero in on what is important in your personal life and your business life. With the right encouragement, yourself and your team can go from muddling by to excelling and, after reading this book, and you will know exactly how to provide the necessary support and encouragement.

As a good coach, you are already aware that poor coaching cannot resolve some issues. If you identify such cases in the course of your engagement, point them out to the parties concerned and recommend appropriate action. In fact, in case you notice your client needs therapy, point it out as best as you can, letting your client know why the coaching will only be beneficial after the treatment. Likewise, if professional consultancy is required, point it out too.

There is a tool for each job and trying to force your coaching tool to help someone suffering, say, depression, cannot get you far. In some African culture they aptly describe such an attempt as trying to groundwater with mortar and pestle – what futility of effort!

Thank you for buying this book it is my sincere hope that you will apply the acquired knowledge productively.